#SOBER NOT B(

APRIL GREEN

#SOBER NOT BORING

How to love living alcohol free.

Copyright 2015 by April Green

No part of this publication may be re-produced, stored in a retrieval system, or transmitted in any form or by any means, electronic, mechanical, photocopying, recording or otherwise, without the prior written permission of the author, nor be otherwise circulated in any form of binding or cover other than that in which it is published and without similar condition being imposed on the subsequent purchaser.

ISBN-13:978-1514316955

DEDICATION

To my beautiful Daughter, who has always loved me and always believed in me.

May your path in life shine brighter than the brightest star.

BOOKS BY APRIL GREEN

#SOBER NOT BORING
how to love living alcohol free

JUST THE TONIC
uplifting quotes, thoughts and exercises to help you stop drinking alcohol

A SOBER SPIRIT
"how do I stop drinking?"
Conversations from the heart

EARTHSONG
poetry and reflections

APRIL GREEN

April Green is a writer who lives in York, and has published three self-help books about overcoming addiction to alcohol.

After losing both parents to cancer within a year of each other, April underwent treatment herself for breast cancer. During this time, April became qualified in Reiki and started studying spirituality and alternative healing techniques, whilst still advocating conventional medical treatment first.

In the six years following her treatment for breast cancer, the only thing clouding April's unyielding, positive outlook on life, was alcohol. When she finally decided to say goodbye to alcohol, every spiritual technique she had learned in those six years, arose and said hello.

April writes with healing passion and is committed to helping others discover their inner spirit; comparing it to a garden, and sharing techniques on how to prepare it for an abundance of bloom.

INTRODUCTION

"A cage went in search of a bird" - Franz Kafka

The above quote is exactly what alcohol did to me.

Alcohol trapped me in a cage for twenty years. It robbed me of my creative freedom; it gave me an inability to love anyone, including myself, and it almost destroyed my relationship with my daughter. Even breast cancer did not deter me from drinking; in fact, it gave me another excuse to drink even more.

When I finally found the key to the cage, I also found that it opened a hidden doorway into a secret garden. I can now see and feel the wood on the trees. I can hear the rain on the sea. I can see the miracle of a single flower; but more importantly, I have learnt how to love and let go. I found the little bird girl deep within me who was buried beneath layers of guilt, sorrow, pain and suffering; and I set her free. Every day, she gets stronger and stronger and flies that little bit further and the cage is now but a dot on the beautiful landscape of life.

This book has been written to help set free the little bird inside you; the spirit you were born as. Because this spirit is all that you are and all that you deserve to be.

If you think that by stopping drinking you are giving something up and that your life will be boring, then look again. Always look again. My life changed beyond words when I found the key to the cage. What took me so long to understand was that I had locked myself in this cage, without realising the key was in front of me all along.

I believed for so long that I would not be happy without alcohol, that I developed an attachment to it, and I convinced myself that I would be unhappy without it. I clung to it and fought off every possibility of losing it. This clinging, or attachment, gave me an emotional dependence on it so that when I received it, I felt pleasure and when I was deprived of it, I felt anxious. I became a prisoner to alcohol and I started re-arranging my life to revolve around it. So, instead of living a joyful, happy life, I started to experience a life of frustration, anger, anxiety and fear.

If I can walk away, after twenty years, without looking back, then so can you. I understand how you feel because I have been there myself. The only reason it seems beyond you now is because you *think* it is and because you *think* it is, you are keeping yourself in the darkest part of the cage.

This book will teach you how to find the key, open the door and step outside, to the place where you have always belonged.

"Love: take me to the place within me I call home." – *April Green*

#Sober Not Boring

THE KNIGHT IN SHINING GLASS

"Loving you was the most exquisite form of self-destruction" – Unknown

When people ask me why, at forty three, I am still single, I always say "I just haven't met the one". In truth, I did meet the one, but he was disguised in the form of a bottle and he controlled my life for twenty years.

I put him before everything else and everyone else, including my daughter. I was loyal, obedient; I spent thousands of pounds on him. I wallowed in the pain and suffering he offered me on a daily basis. Even days without him were spent thinking about the next time he would consume me.

Sometimes I would be disloyal and choose his weaker counterparts. That way, the pleasure lasted longer and the pain the next day was never as bad. But I would put on too much weight with them and their weakness just didn't appeal to me after a while. I missed his strength and paradoxically, I missed the painful stain he left in my body the next day; his faint smell on my skin, his odour on my breath. I was anxious when I was with him and I was panic stricken without him.

The power he had over me became impenetrable. I tried to break free and into the arms of real men, but his hold over me was just too powerful. I would hide him upstairs, in the bathroom, in my bedroom, anywhere I could, to be able to sneak away and taste him, quickly and destructively. Alas, you can't have two lovers; not under that same roof anyway. One always wins. And for me, it was always the faithful one who stood by me through thick and thin, the one who never complained, only spoke through me and never said no.

THE HOLE IN MY SOUL

"Unlearning – the greatest gift we can be taught" – April Green

From as far back as I can remember something never felt right.

I was different; a rebel, a twin, an attention seeker. I had a "hole in my soul" and a deep yearning for something. I didn't know what it was, but it was something. And I could never get enough of anything in my quest for searching for the "something."

I always wanted more. More love, more drama, more attention and more pain. I developed a false belief that without all of these things, I could not possibly be happy.

When I tried alcohol for the first time, my inner world changed and I suddenly felt "whole." I then swallowed another false belief – "without alcohol, I was half a person and could not possibly be happy."

I now understand that I was born with a genetic predisposition towards alcoholism. My progression into the disease was quick, dramatic and destructive, much like my relationships. I acknowledged alcohol was a problem for me early on and I regularly had periods of abstinence. I just didn't know what I know now:

Nothing or no-one can **make** us happy. We make ourselves happy.

And my attachment to the false beliefs I had set up for myself since childhood, caused me the most indescribable unhappiness and darkness you can imagine.

When I finally understood that happiness was a frame of mind that we can all find within us, I also realised that the choice to break free was within me, not outside of me.

And I was in control of the choice.

THE HIDDEN TRUTH

"I am terrified by this dark thing that sleeps in me" – Sylvia Plath

Why did I understand early on in my drinking life that alcohol was going to be a problem for me?

I drank much quicker than most people. I became irritated at how slow people drank. I couldn't understand how some people could make a glass of wine last all night and *then* have a cup of tea.

If my bottle was running low, I panicked at the thought of it becoming empty.

I started buying extra and hiding it in my bedroom, making regular excuses to go and touch up my make-up (which I invariably did, but not before swigging from the hidden bottle).

When I poured the last glass and had no more wine in the house, I had to either get some more (which usually entailed making an excuse to go to the shop and driving well over the limit) or going to bed, (even if it was only eight o clock).

I preferred drinking alone than in the company of others where my speed of consumption would be highlighted. If I drank in company, I would always top up my glass using little bottles of wine I had brought along in my handbag, whenever anyone left the room.

I was aware I had a different "relationship" with alcohol than my friends.

I started to hate everything about alcohol but I started to hate everything about myself even more.

The feeling of loneliness, emptiness and complete and utter self-loathing started to consume me and alcohol started to keep me company.

LONELINESS

"Loneliness: the relationships I forced for fear of being alone." – April Green

We are never alone with a bottle of wine or any drink of our choice. We are always in a fantasy world; re-living the dead past or envisioning a better future. We go over the same conversations, the same regrets or the same daydream about the future. No one says "no" in our fantasy world and the past is always played out with a piece of retribution thrown in for good measure and of course, a happy ending.

We cling to our thoughts and truly believe them. Alcohol distorts the truth; our perception of what is actually happening is clouded and blown out of proportion.

Drinking changes you and over time, your drinking changes. I've watched it happen to myself and I've watched it happen to other people. You start to drink earlier and quicker. The hyperactive mood swiftly takes on a darker, depressive, vacant mood. You finish drinking your quota quicker than before and you want more. A bottle that used to last me an evening, was lasting just an hour. Sometimes two large glasses would be consumed within half an hour; that's two thirds of a bottle. No matter how hard I tried to make the bottle last longer, the grip it had over me was overwhelming. It got to the stage where I didn't feel I could even talk to my daughter without having a drink first. Every morning my resolve would be strong (I talk about how to keep it strong all day in a chapter about self-discipline), but come the drive home, I would stop at the shop, hide the drink in my handbag, unlock the front door, go to the toilet, swig a third of the bottle, then go and say hello.

I have spent many a morning in tears, despising myself, cursing myself and promising myself and my daughter that things will change, only to spend a torturous day at work, wishing the day to end, driving to the shop on the way home and doing it all again.

#Sober Not Boring

I know everything about problem drinking. I know that it stems from a problem existing inside of you that sends you searching for an answer or a cure, outside of you. Usually we find something that changes the way we feel. And when something so freely available like alcohol changes the way we feel, we start to chase that feeling and continue trying to change the way we feel. However, all we are actually doing is masking the original problem; burying it deep down and letting it lay heavy on our souls.

PLEASURE Vs PAIN

"You," he said, "are a terribly real thing in a terribly false world, and that, I believe, is why you are in so much pain." – Alice in Wonderland

You do not have to be an alcoholic to have a problem with alcohol. It's the thinking, not the drinking that determines alcoholism in a person, (the hole in the soul). However, it is possible to have a problem with alcohol, even when it has not progressed to the point of alcoholism. I have watched friends get to the stage I was at, but they didn't seem to have the dark side I was born with and this makes me believe that you can be born an alcoholic but you can also become an alcoholic over time. Problem drinking means you drink too much at times, causing repeated problems in your life.

Either way, alcohol will always cause more problems, unless it is consumed in moderation (and stays that way). Deepak Chopra explains moderation perfectly:

"Think of life as a river with two banks – pleasure on one side, pain on the other. The best way to float down that river is to stay in the middle, moving evenly between the two banks. If you stray too close to either side, your passage slows and you run the risk of running aground. Too much pleasure leads to addiction. Too much pain can eclipse your enjoyment of life".

The perfect way for anyone to live their life is by swimming in the middle of the river. This is a good question to ask yourself about all aspects of your life: Am I swimming in the middle? Which side am I too close to? Sometimes you need to step outside, get some air and remind yourself to keep swimming in the middle. In the early days of my recovery, if something bothered me at work, I would often go to the toilet and just stand there and say to myself "Well done April, look at what you have achieved. That's all that matters at the moment. Keep swimming in the middle. Don't forget". After all the things I had been through, this simple act of self-encouragement was so profound at times.

I will never forget the shame and pain I felt when I was at work, in the grip of my addiction. Hiding behind my mask of immaculate hair and make-up, I would witness life going on around me as though I was watching a play. Not a single person knew the pain I was experiencing; the physical pain of a hangover, but also the knowledge that I was living a lie, trapped in a cage and letting myself out every day to be able to pay to live, then crawling back in every night to escape reality. The power alcohol had over me was impenetrable. I knew the answer and I knew what I needed to do, but the cage was all I had known for so long, that it felt unfaithful to leave.

Conformity (following the crowd) also plays a big role in how our drinking habits unfold. Following the crowd leads to discontentment because someone will always be doing better than you. Maybe because they didn't follow the crowd; they had a goal and they followed that instead. The crowd followed them.

Drinking too much in order to fit in, often leads to making wrong choices, living with the wrong choices and then drinking more to mask the wrong choices. It then gets to the stage where alcohol starts coming first and our own growth is stunted. Our careers stop progressing, we start working to live, we stop looking after ourselves, we get to the stage where we have no drive to succeed and we question what life is all about; we become depressed. We drink even more and then we get trapped in a vicious cycle and an even darker cage.

I KNOW

I know darkness. Alone with your thoughts is not a good place to be but alone with your thoughts and a bottle of wine is truly bleak when you are a problem drinker.

I know the feeling of the overwhelming compulsion to drink when you know you have an important meeting the next day, the first day in a new job, an early start, a car journey, a date. I know that feeling; the battle between right and wrong which goes on in your head.

I know the feeling of being so excruciatingly hung-over on a Saturday or a Sunday, that the only remedy is to have another drink a few hours before the normal "time".

I know where the bruises I lied about came from.

I know that a bottle of wine fits perfectly into my brown handbag.

I know that wrapping bottles in newspaper stops them from clinking when you throw them in the bin.

I know that four 187ml bottles equal 748mls and a fifth 187ml bottle is one too many and I can smell it the next day. I know that when I drive to get the fifth bottle, I am drunk. I know I bought small with the best intention to keep the consumption small.

I know that when I went home from work at lunchtime for a week, it was to lie down and repair my broken body after falling down the stairs backwards. I know I drank every night that week to ease the pain and dull the memory of the fall.

I know that the only time I was sick during chemo was due to alcohol. I know that I used to take my anti sickness tablets for hangovers.

I know every trick in the book about hiding my drinking and lying.

I know how to act like a victim and blame others including my daughter, for driving me to drink.

I know the torturous feeling of running out of alcohol when you're nowhere near ready to call it a night, and you can't get hold of any more. This happened to me in Venice when I was away with friends celebrating the end of breast cancer treatment. Two of us shared a bottle of wine with our meal and then headed back to the resort where I silently assumed a local shop would be open to buy more alcohol (even though it was a Sunday in Italy).

The ferry was delayed by an hour and the journey back was half an hour on top. I needed another drink! The torture was excruciating. For anyone who doesn't have a problem with alcohol, this torment is incongruous. It doesn't make any sense. But when you have an addiction to alcohol, not having any alcohol when you have already had some, is torture. The only thing I can compare this to is giving a happy baby some milk and then taking it away from them after only one minute. They were quite content without it, but the minute you tempted them with it, you opened up a desire for more. With alcohol, the only way this feeling leaves you, is when you have had too much, you are too tired and you pass out in bed. The other way is to abstain from drinking in the first place.

When we got back to the resort the shop was closed so I put myself to bed early and spent a sleepless few hours in hell.

YOU DON'T DRINK THAT MUCH!

I know what people have said to you in the past:

"Stop being such a drama queen, you don't drink that much, just get it under control. You're not an alcoholic; you don't drink in the morning. Only weak people are alcoholics. Can't you just have one? Slow down; just takes sips. Enjoy it. Oh don't be silly, we had a great night. It's Friday! You work hard; you deserve a drink. You're only young once; life's too short. You will be boring sober.

I can hear them now. But, can they hear your thoughts? Do they live in your head?

Other people have a burning desire to be right. Their desire to be right and "know better" than you is dismissive and disrespectful. It simply compounds low self-esteem.

And here is an insight for you. Their lack of understanding may be due to lack of knowledge or it may be due to their own issues; their own unhappiness. BUT – it is probably down to their own attachment to false beliefs – "without something or someone outside or you, you cannot be happy."

You **can.** This is about you and only you. This is about unlearning **your** beliefs and developing new ones.

I want to show you how to unlock the cage and begin to live and love. I know what stops us from unlocking the cage. I know how to tap into the power within and keep that power abundant. I know that you too can do this and transform your life to the one that you deserve to have.

This is an uplifting book from now on and you can choose the ending.

It takes courage to face this road of self-discovery but I promise it will be worth it. The alternative is to carry on living with pain and cage fever; not able to develop your creative potential; not able to grow spiritually and

#Sober Not Boring

mentally; not able to set goals and reach them, and worst still, staying chained to the cage and calling it a life.

A BLESSING IN DISGUISE

"Every experience, no matter how bad it seems, holds within it a blessing of some kind. The goal is to find it"- Buddha

When I was diagnosed with breast cancer I drank even more. The excuse of course, was that I felt entitled to. I could do what I wanted, plus it was helping me get through the shock of losing a breast and facing months of treatment.

But then something happened. I didn't die. In spite of my Dad, then my Mum dying from cancer fifteen months and two months respectively, before my diagnosis, I didn't die. I drank like a fish, but I didn't die.

What I discovered was a passion for gaining spiritual knowledge, for Reiki, crystals, meditation and metaphysics (the power of thought). When I finally unlocked the cage of alcohol addiction six years later, this knowledge came into practice in the form of understanding the subconscious mind, the ego, the spirit and the secret behind affirmations, in the role of addiction and then recovery.

It is said that every problem has a hidden blessing and breast cancer was a blessing for me because without it, I would not have found freedom from alcohol addiction. I would not have understood the true gift of life and how to properly use this gift. It was free after all. In fact "the best things in life are free"; we just have to learn how to see them. We cannot see behind a mask.

The saddest thing about being an active alcoholic is the pain behind the mask. It's difficult to explain to a normal drinker the degree of suffering and self-loathing we carry with us in the midst of our addiction. It feels like we are encased in a vice like grip, completely at the mercy of alcohol.

#Sober Not Boring

I feel sad for emotional eaters because they too must carry this heaviness, on top of the extra weight that they hide behind. Any addict for that matter. It's a lonely place to live.

The hardest thing to do is make the decision to stop. It can take months, years and sometimes one may never make it.

But sometimes your Achilles heel is the very thing that will carry you in the right direction and when I took away the alcohol, I not only took away the problems but I opened up a doorway leading to a magical garden.

Once you make the decision, the mist clears, the sun shines and life begins. Sober people are happy! We look years younger; our weight reduces and remains stable, and so do our emotions. We know a secret and we want to shout it from the rooftops.

IF NOTHING EVER CHANGED, THERE WOULD BE NO SUMMER

"Your desire to change must be greater than your desire to stay the same"
- Unknown

Whenever I've gone on a diet, I've stuck to it. No cheating, no problem. Why? Because my desire to lose weight and look good, was stronger than my desire to stay the same.

With alcohol, whenever I've stopped, I've given in to temptation after a few days, a few weeks and even a few months. Why? Because for me, alcohol was an addictive drug and I saw the past through rose tinted glasses. I forgot where it had taken me and I thought that by going back, I would become a normal drinker again. The addictive part of alcohol was clouding my vision, at all times.

So why this time around, do I know in my heart and soul that I will never go back? What knowledge did I unlock this final time around?

I realised I was being controlled;

I learned the difference between ego and spirit (bad wolf and good wolf) and their role in addiction and recovery;

I worked out what was holding me back;

I started to understand the power of the subconscious mind;

I discovered the secret to affirmations and why they don't work for so many people;

I decided to change my mind-set;

I accepted I couldn't drink alcohol and I became non-attached;

I learned the art of being present;

I learned how to become self-disciplined;

#Sober Not Boring

I started weight lifting;

I started making goals;

I discovered I had unused potential;

I started to like myself;

I started to LOVE living.

BEING CONTROLLED

"What consumes your mind, controls your life" - *Unknown*

I feel sad when I look back at the pain and suffering I went through at the clutches of alcohol. I was a slave to alcohol and alcohol controlled every aspect of my life. I feel sad when I watch people being controlled by such a powerful drug.

Nothing should over power us in life. We should all be free. "Salute no man along the highway" is a saying I use to remind myself that no one is bigger or better than me. I may work for somebody, but they are not bigger than me. We should have no masters in our lives; we are not slaves.

Why then did I pay for something to *become* so much bigger and powerful than me? Why did I pay for something to make decisions for me? (Often wrong ones at that). Why did I pay with not just money, but at the expense of my spirit, my relationship with my daughter and even my breast? (Scientific evidence suggests that alcohol can contribute to breast cancer)

The reason I allowed something to control me was because my drinking had got out of control. I was addicted to alcohol and it began to consume my mind and control every emotion going. If something bad happened I would drink in an attempt to forget; if something good happened, I would drink in order to celebrate; and if nothing happened, I would drink to make something happen. I couldn't control any aspect of my life without having a drink. I was hooked.

Some people genuinely believe they are in control and the thought of stopping never crosses their mind (because they are in control). Even if they tried, they would end up pouring the drink because they made the choice to do that, therefore they must be in control.

#Sober Not Boring

I have heard someone say that they control their drinking because they never want to be in a position to *have* to stop. To me, that says they are already aware that their drinking has gotten out of control. They think they are in charge and that if *they* decide exactly when they can drink, then they are in control, not the other way around. However, on the days in between the "allowance" days, they will be tormented with the thought of alcohol. I have been there and it's not a good way to live week by week.

The days between drinking are usually wished away so that you can get to your permitted "date night". When something challenging happens, the date night gets brought forward. When something good happens, the date night gets brought forward. For me, the only cure for this horrible on the bandwagon, off the bandwagon feeling, was abstinence.

The idea of stopping for good, was working its way out of my subconscious mind for many, many months. The little bird girl was just getting more and more fed up of the pain she was enduring and the suffocation she was feeling.

The day before I stopped was a day that started perfectly and should have stayed that way. It was just before Christmas and my Daughter and I were travelling to Leeds so that she could buy herself a watch she had spent months saving up for. Her face was a picture of pride when she handed over her hard saved money in exchange for a watch encased in a gift box and placed into a designer bag.

Once the watch purchase was ticked off the list, I decided that a trip to Harvey Nichols to celebrate would be the next stop. As usual, I found any excuse for having a glass of wine, plus my hangover from the night before was causing me anxiety and the only way to feel "normal" was to have another drink. I knew the excuse to drink was the addiction talking and I knew *it* was in control.

For some reason that day, the look on my Daughter's face when I ordered a large Prosecco had a greater impact on me than before. Perhaps she felt more of an adult because she had made her first big purchase of something tangible, or perhaps she just knew that a perfect day was about to come to an end and result in me drinking a bottle of wine once we'd arrived home. Whatever it was, I felt more shame than ever before. I felt weak, I felt embarrassed and I looked exactly those things.

You see, after just one glass, I would go somewhere. In other words, I would lose my sense of presence; I would drift off; lose my ground and my focus and start to daydream. I would become impatient and irritable with any kind of distraction such as her little voice attempting to make conversation, on a bar stool in Harvey Nichols, with an expensive watch in her bag and a lush for a Mum by her side. Defiantly I have another glass before we leave and by that stage my eyes are bloodshot and I'm yawning and looking "smudged" as I call it. The day was ruined the second I took a sip of wine because that one sip led to a swift consumption of more.

I wonder how I would feel as a fifteen year old, walking around Leeds, had my Mum done the same. Would I be terrified in case she falls over, we get lost, we miss the train or if she wanted to stop somewhere and have another drink? (It did cross my mind). Things start to get fuzzy for me after a couple of large glasses – almost a bottle that is. You think no-one can tell you've had a drink, however when you stop and watch the effect just one glass has on someone, let alone a bottle, you will be very surprised, and ashamed. You think you are able to hide it, but that's far from the truth. The effect wine has on someone stands out like a sore thumb to someone who hasn't had a drink.

The train home was tempered with the usual "shall I, shan't I" when the drinks trolley arrived, however the only thing that stopped me was the drive home from the station, which of course was already over the limit for me. It still didn't stop me picking up a bottle of Cava from the corner shop.

And that was it; the last time I drank alcohol. Nothing disastrous had happened, (not compared to where alcohol had taken me before anyway). I just decided that I was sick and tired of feeling sick and tired. I had spoiled a day that should have been perfect, and this made me realise I had been spoiling every day of my life with the same, self-destructive behaviour.

I got up the next morning for a doctor's appointment for an ear infection, smelling of wine and feeling tearful that I couldn't even remember what my daughters watch looked like let alone what else we had bought. When I got into the surgery with no makeup on, unwashed hair, mismatched clothes and anxiety, I realised my life had become one massive, unmanageable mess. I was not in control and I asked for help.

That was the day I stepped off the downward escalator and decided to fly the rest of the way home. That was the day I completely and utterly understood that alcohol was in charge and that I had lost control. I had absolutely no doubt about this. I was NOT in control. I was defeated and then I won. The acceptance of defeat made me a winner. But not before I looked at what else had been holding me back.

THE VOICE IN MY HEAD

"People don't want to hear the truth, because they don't want their illusions destroyed". Friedrich Nietzsche

If you are reading this book because you are worried about your drinking then you have already started listening to the little voice inside you. This little voice has called you by your name and asked you to get help. Listening to this voice is the best choice you have made so far. Why? Because this voice is your true self, your spirit, the little bird trapped under layers of self-loathing, denial, fear and guilt. This voice speaks only the truth. Deep down, you already know the truth.

You are no longer in control. But sometimes, there is a deeper truth.

Sometimes we use alcohol to mask the truth. Sometimes the truth is colder than a lie and we don't want to bring it to the surface. We therefore keep drowning it in alcohol.

Your truth may be that you do not like, let alone love yourself. You are lonely. You are unhappy in your relationship. You are unfulfilled at work. You are living a lie.

Drowning your truth with alcohol will only cause it to get bigger and lay heavier at the bottom of your soul. But you need to know from me, that there is treasure to be found at the bottom of your soul.

There comes a time when you have to let your truth wash up to the shore; over your heart and out from your eyes so that you can face it and then make friends with it. If you would rather keep it buried deep, then please understand that it will not go away.

So what's your truth? Dwell on this question and let your spirit tell you the answer. You will hear the soft voice of truth answering you. Try to understand that the voice within you that speaks gently and calls you by your name "April, please stop drinking" is the voice that loves you. So what does your spirit voice keep telling you?

My truth was many. I didn't like the person I was. I felt unworthy of love. I was lonely. I married to conform instead of to love. I married because my biological clock was ticking and I wanted a child. I drank because I was living a lie and because I was living a lie, I drank. I went into relationships to try and fill emptiness. Hence, I went into relationships for personal gain. I now understand that gains lie within and not without (on the inside of you and not from something or someone on the outside of you). Once you get your head around this very old, meaningful saying, you will start to understand something very important. Gains lie within. And once you fill up from within, your outside life becomes full. Life is just a mirror, what you give out, you get back. It is fun to start watching what unfolds in your life when you realise you are thinking your life from within. If you are thinking you are depressed then you will see more things to make you feel depressed. If you are thinking you are lucky then you will see more things to feel lucky about. There is more of this in the second half of the book.

However, there is also another voice that talks to you and usually takes control over the spirit voice and this is the voice of ego (bad wolf, devil, chimp, man on your shoulder) and this sabotages all of your good intentions. There is a reason why ego is so powerful and it is because it is addicted to the things you are doing to yourself and it is afraid of change. Even now, it will be telling you to "close this book; you do not have a drink problem - have another drink!" It will not diminish until you acknowledge and accept it as an imposter. This imposter lives off fear, and in turn, feeds you false evidence appearing real; in order to keep you under his control. You were not born to be a slave, but this pretender takes you into his cage the minute he smells fear.

THE BAD WOLF

"Rule your mind or it will rule you". Buddha

An old Cherokee told his Grandson, "My Son, there is a battle between two wolves inside us all. One is Evil. It is anger, jealousy, greed, resentment, inferiority and lies. The other is good. It is joy, peace, love, hope, humility, kindness, empathy and truth".

The boy thought about it, and asked "Grandfather, which wolf wins?"

The old man quietly replied "The one you feed".

The only reason you have been swept under the current of alcohol and stayed there for so long, is because you believed the thoughts that alcohol fed you in order to keep you in its cage and by continuing to drink, you are feeding these thoughts. It has made you afraid of a life without it but paradoxically, deep down, you are afraid of a life with it. If I told you that fear should stand for "false evidence appearing real" would you start to understand that most of your thoughts aren't actually real? The bad wolf makes you really believe that you are worthless and that your life can't get any better than it is.

Alcohol changes the way you think and it makes all that you are thinking, appear real. Even when you are not drinking, the wolf starts to get hungry throughout the day and starts to tell you that having a drink will make things much better. However, they only appear better because you believe the thought that he has tempted you with. You also believe the thought that tonight you will just have one drink. If this isn't false evidence appearing real then I don't know what is.

I used to have the good intention of "just one drink" every night when I was drinking. What does this good intention tell you? It tells you that you really don't want to get drunk tonight and it tells you that after just one sip, your resolve is out the window; something much bigger has been fed. The way you think has literally changed in just a few seconds.

#Sober Not Boring

The bad wolf, or ego, devil, man on your shoulder, is afraid that if it doesn't think, it will get bored and cease to exist. It is attracted to novelty and therefore searches frantically for interesting thoughts and sensations. These interesting thoughts usually come tenfold as a result of drinking alcohol.

Boredom is relatively easy to get over simply by seeing that boredom is just frustration of not being amused by interesting thoughts.

When we drink, we are literally feeding the bad wolf. The more we feed it, the bigger it becomes. This is why we become egotistical when we drink. Our ego (bad wolf) has been fed. We become arrogant, self-absorbed and not very interested in anyone but ourselves. Look closely at the fantasies you have in your drink fuelled daydream. Are you the main character; are you the one with power? The term "big headed" refers to the bad wolf. And it won't go away until we learn to accept it as an imposter; a shadow not belonging to us, which simply sits alongside us and can easily be dissolved by simply ceasing to feed it. Have you also noticed that if someone becomes argumentative when they drink they usually say the next day: "You've got to understand, it wasn't really me". No, it was ego. Whenever I am with a drinker and this happens, I am actually quite forgiving the next day. One, because I have been there myself, and two because I understand they have woken up a sleeping wolf. It doesn't mean that becoming argumentative is acceptable though, especially if they keep repeating the same behaviour then using the same "it wasn't me" excuse.

"When we repeat a mistake, it's not a mistake anymore; it's a decision" –
Paulo Coelho

We drink because we want our lives to get better. We think that external circumstances have caused our lives to turn out the way they are, however I can assure you that your life has not turned out this way because of a set of circumstances or by things that have happened to you. They have turned out this way because you have become addicted to a drug that feeds a bad wolf that lives off the pain and suffering of negative thinking. Unless you accept that your thoughts are the cause of everything in your life, good and bad, you will continue to seek the cause outside of you, and never find the answer.

Nothing has ever come into your life uninvited. I will repeat this, because when I understood this statement, it changed the way I looked at everything! **Nothing has ever come into your life uninvited**.

By using alcohol to dull the reality of your situation, you are actually feeding negative thoughts and making your situation appear much worse. You are literally inviting pain and suffering into your life. The main cause of unhappiness is never the situation, but our thoughts about it. We act as though it is us against the world, whereas it is really just us against ourselves by believing that our thoughts are real.

You are what you think and alcohol makes you think differently; it makes you think negatively, it sugar coats the truth to keep you in its grip and it hides the miracle of life behind very dark clouds.

FALSE EVIDENCE APPEARING REAL (FEAR)

"Sometimes, the thing you're most afraid of doing is the very thing that will set you free" - Unknown

The feeling of waking up that first day of my new life cannot be put into words.

The secret is to feel excited about it. Feel that you really have found the key and opened the cage door, because that is exactly what you have done.

So what is holding you back? Be truthful with yourself.

Are hangovers holding you back? Do you enjoy them and want them to continue? Is wasting money holding you back? Do you enjoy throwing money down the drain? Is the stubborn weight you always seem to be carrying holding you back? Are you scared to lose weight? Is living in the past holding you back? Do you enjoy dwelling on the past and fantasising about the future, or rather about controlling the future?

Or is it fear? Is the bad wolf feeding you so much fear that you honestly believe:

Your life will be boring;

You are giving something up.

Are you boring during the day when you are at work? Are you boring in the morning? Are you boring when you meet a friend for coffee? Or is it that you *think* you enjoy life more when you are drinking? Is it just the thought that it will be boring? Have you tired stopping before and why did you try it? Was it really boring or did too many people tell you it was, or did you just not give it a chance? Did you have a boring night because you were forced to drive, or couldn't drink for a reason? Then it probably was boring because all you were focusing on was the wanting to drink because you knew you couldn't. It wasn't really your choice and because of that, it felt like deprivation.

Your senses actually get heightened when you stop drinking. When you are out with friends, you see and absorb *everything*. You feel real laughter, you hear the music in the background, you listen to people, and you remember *everything*. This is not boring, this is enlightening. The greatest gift you can give somebody is to actually listen to them. You become a much better, humble person when you listen. Boring is talking about yourself nonstop. Boring is talking *at* people. Boring is talking about the past so that you don't have to focus on the present, which is real. Boring is talking about the past to try and make people in the present moment feel inferior. Boring is trying to impress people by showing off about the people you have met, the things you have done, the places you have visited, the money you earn. The evil wolf is one big, bad, boring beast!

Being boring sober is just an illusion alcohol gives us to keep us in its grip. An illusion is false evidence appearing real which equals fear, which is exactly what the bad wolf lives off.

Drinkers started the rumour that being sober is boring. Sober people certainly didn't start that rumour! We don't need to go around shouting about it either, because we have stopped feeding the bad wolf therefore we have dissolved our egos and our arrogance and we are quietly confident with our choices and the way our lives have turned around. We have stopped seeking approval. We have stopped trying to impress people. We are no longer weak and living a lie so there is no need to impress. The very fact that we have found the key is impressive enough.

In fact, so many negative character traits start dissolving when you stop drinking and sometimes you don't even notice. You just start to feel that you are a better person. You are at peace. It's a wonderful feeling. Self-doubt stops, negative thinking stops, fear of failure stops, criticising yourself and others stops, negative self-talk stops, procrastination stops, and people pleasing stops. I could say that it should be bottled and sold, but it is actually free and waiting for you to discover for yourself.

#Sober Not Boring

So let's go on to the second thing that is stopping you. You *think* you are giving something up.

Don't forget that unless the thought is coming from deep within you, your thoughts are usually false. They are illusions, they are not real; they are false. You are giving up the very thing that causes you so many problems in your life. You are walking away from the controlling knight in shining glass.

Would you walk away from a knight in shining armour who was going to lift you up onto his stallion and take you to a land where you would become wealthier, slimmer, healthier and full of self-love, self-discipline, and self-respect? Now, I certainly wouldn't walk away from him! But a poisonous knight in shining glass who cuts my wounds, gives me headaches, makes me sick, makes me angry, sad, lonely, fat, bloated, non-ambitious, neglectful, the list goes on. Wow, I am certainly giving him up, I can tell you!

This is just the beginning of weight loss, good health, more money, better skin, sparkling eyes, youthfulness, self-respect, and happiness. You can have all this in abundance and more, if you get your head around the fact that you are not losing out on anything by giving up alcohol. The reason you think every day seems the same, is because you have stopped noticing the miracles contained in every day. I had stopped noticing because I was not present; I was drunk and I was living in the past and worrying about the future.

You can have all this in abundance and more, if you get your head around the fact that you are not losing out on anything by giving up alcohol. The reason you think every day seems the same, is because you have stopped noticing the miracles contained in every day.

I had stopped noticing because I was not present; I was drunk and I was living in the past and worrying about the future.

The following is from an unknown and depicts precisely what the knight in shining glass does to us:

"I drank for happiness and became unhappy. I drank for joy and became miserable. I drank for sociability and became argumentative. I drank for sophistication and became obnoxious. I drank for friendship and made enemies. I drank for sleep and woke up tired. I drank for strength and became weak. I drank for relaxation and got the shakes. I drank for courage and became afraid. I drank for confidence and became doubtful. I drank to make conversation easier and slurred my speech. I drank to feel heavenly and ended up feeling like hell".

Giving something up when you are going to lose everything would be very tough. Giving something up when you will gain in abundance and more is a no brainer. Sorry to be blunt but I am just trying to teach you what I wish I had been taught years ago.

It may seem like the hardest thing to absorb right now, but only because you are in the grip of an addiction and you believe your thoughts and the thoughts of other drinkers. Listening to your bad wolf is bad enough but listening to other bad wolves is suicide.

The very fact that you can't see the gain goes to show just how clouded your mind is. We have too often been conditioned to see that emotional surrender to something, even something as negative as a drug, is a loss and not a gain. In just three days the physical addiction to alcohol will have left your body. In just three weeks, the clouds will start to lift. In just three months, you will be a different person and you will hopefully never look back. The reason I feel so passionately about this is because I have been to hell and I was unable to see how to get to heaven. I was listening to the bad wolf. (And everyone else's bad wolf). If hell was better, then trust me, I would still be there. I would still be in the dark cage. But then I wouldn't be ten pounds lighter, I wouldn't look ten years younger and I wouldn't have been able to see myself and my daughter transform in front of my eyes.

A saying I really love is: "if you keep doing what you're doing, you will keep getting what you get".

#Sober Not Boring

Maybe there is a piece of you that is happy with what you are getting. But I ask you, where is this piece? Where is it speaking from? Is it speaking from your soul or your bad wolf?

By breaking a habit, you are choosing to set yourself free and fly into a kingdom you have forgotten exists. Don't live the same day or week a hundred times over and call it a life. The first day of your life starts when you understand you are no longer in control, the bad wolf is supplying you with fear, you will be anything but boring and you are giving up NOTHING and gaining EVERYTHING.

PART TWO

THE SECRET GARDEN

"What if I fall? Oh, but my darling, what if you fly? - Erin Hanson

The day I left the doctors surgery, I was armed with two things: freedom and a phone number for Lifeline.

Those two things started a transformation I never believed possible. I had admitted I was no longer in control and by simply becoming aware of this, the feeling of being out of control diminished. My spirit; my core, took control.

When I phoned Lifeline, I had to wait two weeks before I could get an appointment. I am sure they would have seen me earlier had I stated I was at crisis point but in truth, I was suddenly at peace. Simply by admitting defeat, acknowledging I was not in control, and seeking help, I had already found the answer. I had gained control. If I was strong enough to do this for myself, then I was strong enough to dissolve the addiction by simply changing my mind.

Everything I had learned and studied in the six years following breast cancer was sitting there waiting for me to put into practice. How blinded I had been. The fog of addiction was so thick that I had been completely stuck in the thick of it. The things I had studied to help me stay breast cancer free were also there to help me become addiction free.

It only takes three days for the physical addiction to alcohol to leave your body. However, if you have understood that you were not in control, that the bad wolf was feeding you with fear, and that you will be giving up nothing but pain and heartache, then these three days should be a breeze. If you're still not convinced then the next half of the book should help.

For me, it was a breeze. Some rocks are just too heavy to carry, and I had spent too many years carrying a heavy rock that I felt instantly

#Sober Not Boring

transformed. But there were also some paradoxes; some feelings I found hard to describe. One minute my life was being wished away, and then suddenly everything slowed down. There was rawness, but also a feeling of renewal. Vulnerability, but also an air of confidence. My voice no longer sounded like mine, (mine, as in drunk, incoherent and loud). Everything slowed down very quickly. The drug that kept me going, (even the pain of a hangover kept me going) suddenly evaporated. And there I was, like a child again. So I started to let my spirit nourish me and carry me. It loved me and wanted to heal me.

When we stop drinking we feel exposed. We feel raw, bare and oversensitive. This is the start of re-birth. Sometimes we have to be brave and walk naked like this for some time before we start to grow again; before we start to learn how to fill ourselves up with goodness and eradicate all the untruths that alcohol gave us. The worst thing we can do at this stage is feel cold and put our old clothes back on.

This feeling reminded me of a lovely story I once read about a man who visited Spain and brought back a beautiful, rare, wild bird. He put the bird in a cage, fed it, gave it water and cared for it. When he went back to Spain, he visited the bird's friends and told them the bird was in a cage, being well looked after. On hearing this, one of the birds dropped dead on the spot. When the man got home he told the bird his friend had died. The bird listened to the story and then he too dropped dead. The man was aghast with grief and took the bird outside to bury it in the garden. On reaching the outside, the bird came back to life and flew onto the branch of a tree. The man asked "my friend, why did you do that?" and the bird replied "because I realised I had to die first before I could be free to live".

My Doctor told me I was brave quitting before Christmas, but timing means nothing when you are in such a dark place. Sometimes there is never a good time. When you've had enough, you've had enough.

Maybe I had to become completely defeated before that last bit of strength, the flame of my spirit, gave me that final spark to do the right thing and ask for help.

I was lucky I was on holiday from work for another week. I had no drive home in the evening and no corner shop to drive past. My routine changed for a week and it is amazing how quickly you can change a neural pathway in your brain in such a short space of time.

Just recently, my work car park was closed for two weeks and I had to park in a temporary location. After just two weeks, I still drove to my temporary location even when the car park was re-opened. I did this again for the next two days. In just two weeks, I had created a new pattern without really trying.

If you decide to stop, then in the first few days I would recommend the following:

Clear your house of any alcohol;

If you usually pick up alcohol on the way home from work, then drive home a different route in the evening;

Nip out at lunch to get your daily essentials instead of waiting until after work. Throw in a few treats for yourself, a cream cake, a bar of chocolate, a magazine, coconut water, sweets.

Go to the cinema or somewhere you can't drink;

Go out for a meal and have a 660 calorie dessert (the same calories as a bottle of wine).

Take some time off work and have three days recovering in peace. You have probably taken time off with a hangover, take time off without one for a change!

If you usually go home and spend the evening downstairs, then go upstairs. My bedroom has always been my haven and I spend a lot of time reading and watching films on top of my bed. Create a new neural pathway and start to go upstairs for the evening – it only needs to be for a few days. If you have a partner and a family, tell them you have a migraine and that you want no interruptions. It's times like this when it's necessary to think about yourself. It's only for a few days. You need to strengthen your resolve.

Sleep. As Shakespeare said: "Let her sleep for when she wakes, she will move mountains".

Read. As I've mentioned before, boredom is relatively easy to get over simply by seeing that boredom is just frustration of not being amused by interesting thoughts. Reading gives you the interesting thoughts to focus on without allowing the bad wolf to give you the thoughts. Reading allows you to be present and the bad wolf cannot work in the present moment, it simply lives in the past and thrives on the uncertainty of the future.

There is a section and some exercises on being present later. However at the moment, you need to spend the next three days looking after yourself, not thinking very much, and feeling excited by the positive changes you will start to notice, with the biggest one being no hangover!

I could say to you, go shopping, treat yourself, change your hair, get a makeover, get a facial, get a massage, but I really think these three days should be about rest and avoiding public places where you will be reminded of alcohol wherever you go.

Don't feel frightened if you feel slightly agoraphobic. This stayed with me well after the first few days. Try to counterbalance any fear because you don't want the bad wolf to smell fear. Keep your thoughts strong. Praise yourself often, you are brave, you will get stronger, and you are recovering.

Recovery means two things and they can both be applied to stopping drinking:

"A return to a normal state of health, mind or strength".

"The action or process of regaining possession or control of something lost or stolen".

Embrace the struggle in the first few days and let it make you stronger. It won't last forever, I promise. Enjoy these few days; it has taken a lot of courage to shed your skin and start to become who you really are. Be proud and do not be afraid; you have chosen to say goodbye to the many negative consequences of drinking alcohol.

#Sober Not Boring

GOODBYE HANGOVER, HELLO LIFE

"If you are brave enough to say goodbye, life will reward you with a new hello" – Paulo Coelho

There are no negative consequences to stopping drinking alcohol. You literally *are* saying goodbye to something destructive.

I had the start of a cold recently and retched when I was brushing my teeth. The memory of mornings when I was unable to lift my head properly whilst carrying out simple tasks and feeling sick, faint and agitated, came flooding back to me. These physical symptoms are untenable to me now. If you were to ask any heavy drinker, any drug addict or any binge eater, if they enjoy doing what they are doing, I am certain the answer would be no. It's a torturous, vicious cycle but it CAN be broken, I am living proof.

The instant benefit to stopping is the undisturbed sleep and the disappearing hangover, as well as cutting out 650 calories per night and having £5-£10 more in your purse every day (not to mention the other money you are spending on takeaway food and hangover food).

The other instant benefits are:

No more guilt; no more waking up in the morning panic stricken about what you have said or done the night before; no more self-loathing and name calling;

No more feeling sick, retching or being sick;

No more headaches, heartburn, palpitations and dehydration;

No more worrying about whether people at work can smell alcohol on you;

No more excuses for staying indoors at weekends to nurse a hangover;

After just a week or two, you stop *thinking* about alcohol. That horrible pull towards the shop on the way home completely leaves you. This was probably the greatest relief for me. The constant "shall I, shan't I" fight going on in my head – gone! The relief was indescribable.

After just three weeks, the clouds lift, the sun comes out and then life just gets brighter and brighter. The best is yet to come, I promise. There are so many ways to strengthen your resolve and reach the three month mark, whereby you and your life start to transform unrecognisably.

THE SUBCONSCIOUS MIND

"Be careful how you are talking to yourself because you are listening" – Lisa M Hayes

At this very moment, your subconscious mind is telling your body to breathe, it is controlling your heartbeat and it is even healing a cut in your mouth. Your subconscious mind takes orders you give it based on what you believe and accept as true. So when you are drinking alcohol, the truth is distorted and you start believing all the negative thoughts that the bad wolf whispers to you. Your subconscious mind is 30,000 times more powerful than your conscious mind! The subconscious mind really is the spirit within you.

If you insist on saying "I can't stop drinking" you may as well be saying to your subconscious mind "We can't stop drinking". Your subconscious mind will take you at your word and make sure that you will never be in a position to stop drinking because you have just told it that you can't stop. If you insist on saying "I can't afford it" then your subconscious mind will ensure you are never in a position to afford something because you have just told it that "we can't afford it". If you say that diets never work for you, then diets will never work for you.

Your subconscious mind does not have an opinion. It does not have a sense of humour or a filter; it follows your orders, positive or negative. It will not step in and say "Hey April, don't sow that negative thought!" It will reap whatever you place in it.

If in your garden, you planted the seed of a beautiful flower and next to it, the seed of a poison, both will grow if they are watered and tendered. But if take your attention away from the poison and feed only the flower, then the flower will start to bloom. The poison will wither and die. This is similar to the good and bad wolf. The more you focus on the flower, the more it will bloom and sow more seeds of beauty. Hence, you literally "reap what you sow". Whatever images you hold in your subconscious mind, will eventually externalise in your life. I promise you. The image of being healthy and sober must be an image you carry around with you, always. **You need to keep feeding the image of the thing you want and the thing you don't want will wither and die.**

A man and his daughter lived in an apartment block in New York and were talking one day about Yellow Cabs. The daughter said "I can never get a cab outside our block" and the man said "I can always get a cab outside our block". They had both impressed an opinion onto their subconscious minds and made a law (truth) for themselves. If both reversed their statements, the opposite would start to happen.

The same applies to superstitions. The lucky charm you have holds no power, but your belief that it will bring you good luck creates quiet expectancy in the subconscious mind and attracts a lucky situation. The magic power is within your thoughts, not within the lucky charm. This is exactly the same with Friday the thirteenth and walking under ladders.

Two estranged brothers who grew up with an alcoholic Father were reunited one day. One had become an alcoholic and the other had never touched alcohol in his life. When asked what made them choose their paths, they both came up with the same answer:

"Well, my Dad was an alcoholic, so what would you expect?"

They saw it as *they* were. We do not see things as they are; we see things as *we* are. I call this the power of the coin. One side is positive and the other side is negative. There are always two ways of looking at something. Which side do you want to see every day of your life? Some people live with the negative side their whole life. If you have spent a long time indulging in alcohol you are also indulging your subconscious mind with fear, worry, anger, ill health and suffering and this is what you will keep getting. And guess who feeds you this fear? The bad wolf. And guess who feeds the bad wolf? Alcohol. It's a terrifying, vicious circle and it all ends up in your subconscious mind.

The remedy for this is to start thinking about happiness, freedom, beauty, miracles, good food, healthy drinks, and good health. If you continue to drink alcohol then this remedy is useless because if your drinking has become a problem, it is impossible to think about happiness when you are drowning in sorrow.

If you take away the alcohol, then you will be in a better position to stay on the positive side of the coin. Then start to make this type of thinking a habit and you will start to undo all the negative thoughts that you have already impressed on your subconscious mind from years of problem drinking.

Yes, there will be negative days and you may feel as though you are going back to your old thinking habits, but now that you are armed with the knowledge that the coin can be flipped any time you desire; it's quite simply a choice. Trust me on this one. If I can focus on the positive, after years of wallowing in self-pity, then so can you.

I am convinced that self-pity manifested itself from my heart, out into my left breast causing cancer. They say that alcohol contributes to lifestyle diseases such as cancer but maybe our personality type leads to drinking too much alcohol, which leads to negative thinking, which leads to self-pity, which leads to disease. Disease stands for "dis" – "ease"; when your mind and body are not at ease with each other. Whatever the cause, self-pity is probably the worst sin you can carry in the spiritual world. I hope you understand that the spiritual world is the world within you. The world you live by using your thoughts and your spirit. You follow the path from your heart and you do not follow the crowd of bad wolves.

To be spiritual is to be truthful about who you are and to always find the truth in whatever lies in front of you. It's about always going back to the spirit within you and listening to the voice of truth and not the voice of ego. It's about finding the truth in every situation you are handed. For example, when we drink we say sweeping statements such as "this situation has ruined my life". In truth, has it? Has a certain situation *really* ruined your life, or is the bad wolf telling you that "Your life has been ruined; let's create really interesting thoughts out of this situation". Always dig deep down into your soul for the truth. What message has the situation brought you? Is it telling you about a decision you have made whilst under the influence of alcohol, which has then caused a problem in your life? Has the situation ruined your life or are you perhaps fuelling the situation with alcohol and is alcohol in fact ruining your life? What is the truth?

I've made some terrible relationship choices whilst under the influence of alcohol. I've then carried on masking the choices with alcohol, drinking over the cracks, and then blaming the other person for making me unhappy. When in actual fact, I was unhappy when I met them, I was unhappy when I was with them and I was unhappy when I left them. The only time I got happy, was when I left alcohol.

If you get used to asking yourself what the truth really is instead of listening to what the bad wolf is telling you and worst still, what other peoples' bad wolves are telling you, you will start to live in peace.

Back to the subconscious mind - you just need to understand how valuable your subconscious mind is and begin to protect it from any false impressions.

I am a huge fan of music and since I stopped drinking, music has become even more important to me and I now listen to upbeat, happy songs, with only positive messages. This doesn't mean I don't listen to a good old ballad every now and again, it just means that I don't play the same old ballad over and over again on repeat: "I had a dream my life would be, so different from this hell I'm living.." or, "I'm so lonesome I could cry."

My life has stopped playing out as the same record; therefore my taste in music has changed. Listening to the same, sad song on repeat will get carved into the subconscious mind, like grooves on an old record. When I look back on my days before I understood the power of the subconscious mind, I realised how much I was drawn to songs of unrequited love, heartache, loss and pain. It seemed romantic and "deep" to listen to tortured souls singing about being tortured souls. I just didn't realise that I was torturing myself with alcohol and then some more by listening to this kind of music. The same old vicious circles again.

Just before I stopped drinking, a friend of mine introduced me to the music of Nahko Bear and Medicine for the People. This Oregon-native, born a mix of Apache, Puerto Rican and Filipino cultures and adopted into an American family, suffered an identity crisis from an early age. But the unifying power of music entered his life as a healing remedy when he took up the piano aged six. Armed with this new found talent, he set about to bridge the cultural gaps dividing this own psyche and began producing a public, musical journal of his journey towards personal, spiritual and communal healing. I play one of his songs and videos every morning when I am getting ready; it is part of my morning ritual. The song is "Aloha Ke Akua" which loosely translates in Hawaiian (and I touch on the beauty of Hawaiian healing which I discovered when I had breast cancer, in a later chapter) as "The breath of life, the love of God".

This video and song uplifts me, I can tell you. If I could go back twenty years, I wonder how different my life up to this stage, would have turned out had I listened to happier, upbeat songs instead of heartbreak. But luckily, it is never too late.

One thing to remember about the subconscious mind - it has no filter and no sense of humour. Your subconscious mind cannot decipher the difference between true and false and when you are under the influence of alcohol, most of what you think is false. Learn to be the "watchman at the gate" when it comes to your thoughts and make sure you never finish a negative statement. Turn every negative into a positive.

Decide right now that this will be a miraculous year for you. Say it over and over again and don't stop.

As the Buddha said, "There is no path to happiness. Happiness *is* the path". We just have to make happiness a habit and it will sink into our subconscious mind and start to play out on our path. But walking with alcohol creates a heavy haze which makes the path hard to manoeuvre. The journey becomes slower; the weather is always against you. Clear the alcohol induced fog, and you will clear your path, I assure you of this.

THE GOOD WOLF

"What you think, you become. What you feel, you attract. What you imagine, you create". Buddha

This section is about affirmations and I have purposely avoided the term because people (including me until I learned the formula to make them work) have often dismissed them as rubbish. Well guess what? If you think that affirmations are rubbish, what will they become in your mind?

I have a secret to tell you about affirmations, which is why they have not worked for so many people. Affirmations MUST be stated in the present tense.

To state "I shall be well" is admitting you are ill. The universe will continually give you that which is, because it does not see the future, only the present moment. Until you turn this statement around and state "I am well" will you continue to receive the opposite of well. Claim yourself to be unhappy and unhappiness will keep following you around. As long as you keep telling yourself you are unhappy, you will keep being that. Even by claiming "I will one day be happy" is the expectancy of the future, which in the present is admitting you are unhappy NOW. With this in mind, you can basically think yourself happy just by changing your thoughts, even if in reality you feel anything but happy. If you persevere, you WILL become happy because trust me when I say "happiness is a habit", just as drinking and feeling miserable was.

To affirm is to "state that it is true". Your attitude of mind must believe something you say is true, irrespective of any evidence to the contrary, and you will start to change the way you see things.

Another important fact about affirmations which has been overlooked by many is that they have a massive impact on your consciousness. If you keep telling yourself you are unhappy, then you will be conscious of this and you will, in body and mind, start to express unhappiness.

Hence, if you are conscious of drinking too much, or of being an alcoholic, then you will keep drinking. You are literally telling the universe and yourself that you are drinking too much, so that is what you will keep doing. Start to state the opposite (even if it is not yet the reality), believe it will become reality, and you will start to act this out.

"I am sober, I am slim, I am happy". It may take weeks, but it must become a habit, just as regular drinking of alcohol was. I started to say this affirmation months before I finally stopped drinking and then I became sober, slim and happy.

The spiritual term "I am that I am" translates as "I am the thing that I state I am". With this in mind, you need to be very careful about the names you call yourself because you will then start to express those names outwardly. "I am weak", "I am a failure", "I am a bad parent". These are all things I have said to myself whilst in the grip of my addiction. In fact, we say some terrible things to ourselves when we are drinking and again, it's the bad wolf speaking through us to weaken our resolve on trying to live happily.

Have you ever wondered how a rich person can lose it all and then within months become rich again? This is because they have carved into their psyche the fact that they are that which they say they are - rich. Even when they became poor, they still claimed to be rich and so they became that again. Have you ever noticed that a happy person just keeps on getting happier and seems to attract happiness and laughter wherever they go? How do they do it? They have never once allowed the thought of being unhappy to enter into their consciousness. They have probably never once claimed themselves to be unhappy, because guess what? That is exactly what they will express.

Do not give up on stating that which you wish to be because stating it is the only way you become it. I do it every minute of the day. I still say, "I am sober, I am healthy, I am slim, and I am cancer free". If you give up, then you are staying as that which you are, a regular drinker. Keep affirming that which you wish to be, every minute of the day if needs be and you cannot possibly feed the bad wolf. The hunger he has will gradually diminish because you cannot feed two opposites.

If you say "I am weak", first of all, who *told* you that? Secondly and more importantly, who *heard* it? The bad wolf told you it but your subconscious mind, the very spirit of you, heard it. Watch your thoughts. Decide who is feeding you these thoughts and only listen to the positive ones that come from within.

Turn your back on the thing you don't want (alcohol) and face, in your imagination and thoughts, the thing that you do want (sobriety) and the thing that you don't want will disappear. This is a universal law and is explained in the story of Daniel in the lion's den:

Whilst locked in the lion's den (the prison of his mind) Daniel turned his back on the ferocious beasts (his problems) and turned towards the light (his soul within him) and prayed to his Father (his awareness) for freedom.

The lions (problems) became powerless to hurt Daniel because his faith in his vision of freedom was so great that this vision was all he fed.

When you are faced with any impossible problem, such as alcoholism, poverty, sickness or even lions, do as Daniel did and remove your attention from these things and focus only on the opposite using your I AM affirmation. Every problem produces an answer in the form of a desire to have the opposite of the problem. For example, "I am unhappy" has an opposite of "I am happy". This is the thing you must focus on to be free of the problem. Be conscious of the feeling you want to have and the opposite will fade away. By using affirmations all day, every day, you can learn how to feed only the good wolf.

One of my daily affirmations was written by Dr Joseph Murphy and has become a daily mantra I recite whilst putting on my make-up and listening to my knight in shining armour, Nahko Bear. There is something about this affirmation that seems to make me feel energised. And because I feel like this, I become this. "I am energised I am" – we are what we state we are remember?

"Divine order takes charge of my life today and every day. All things work together for me today. This is a new and wonderful day for me. There will never be another day like this one. I am divinely guided all day long and whatever I do will prosper. Divine love surrounds me, enfolds me and enwraps me and I go forth in peace. Whenever my attention wanders away from that which is good and constructive, I will immediately bring it back to the contemplation of that which is lovely and of good report. I am a spiritual and mental magnet, attracting to myself all things which bless and prosper me. I am a wonderful success in all of my undertakings today. I am definitely going to be happy all day long".

I have this written down on a lovely colourful piece of paper and there is something very spiritual about unfolding it every morning, reading it through, reading every single word slowly and feeling very present. It is my morning prayer and I would strongly advise you to do the same and build it in to your daily routine. You will be amazed at how much beauty you start to notice on your journey to work in the morning. Once you start noticing the beauty of the universe, then you will start to realise that you are present and the present moment is really all you ever have. I also changed the last sentence to "I am definitely going to be sober and happy all day long".

Other affirmations I recite throughout the day - the drive to work in the morning, the drive home, before I go to sleep are: "I am loved, I am slim, I am sober, I am healthy, I am safe, I am cancer free" plus, I always add on a "thank you" at the end of every affirmation.

Affirmations must become a habit because they remind you of what you should be focusing on and they keep out the bad wolf. Thoughts repeated regularly, good or bad, submerse themselves into your subconscious mind and start to crystallise into your life.

Happiness is a choice, not a result. In other words, a car, a house, a big salary, does not equal happy. Nothing will make you happy until you choose to be happy. You can change the way you think, you can make a choice to be happy, but if you carry on drinking, that choice will be impossible to reach. Once you take away the alcohol, you take away all the negative thoughts so that the only option you have is to see and think the positive in everything.

At first, it may seem difficult to try and look at things positively because alcohol has trained your mind to think negatively and see life through its eyes. It may seem at first that you have taken away the alcohol, yet the suffering continues. Look again; always look again. Please believe me when I say that the darkness from the cage in which you have been living will start to fade every single day, until the door becomes wide open and the only option you have is to fly.

LET GO OF WHAT YOU CAN'T CHANGE

"Accept what is, let go of what was, believe in what will be" - Buddha

I would like my left breast back, but I accept I can't have it back. I would like my parents back, but I accept I can't have them back. I would like to consume just one glass of wine, and then move onto a cup of tea, but I accept I can't do that. I spent many years suffering with this thought. Abstaining on and off for many years, attempting to "become" a normal drinker, but I finally accepted that I was never that.

Acceptance really is a wonderful thing once you get your head around it. The secret is to stop trying to resist something because in trying to resist, you are focusing on it constantly and when you resist something, it will cause much suffering. Sometimes we think that we resist certain states because they are there, but in truth, they are there because we resist them. If you were holding a balloon and tried to let go of it, then the trying becomes the focus instead of the letting go. Letting go is more like letting be. Some things just cannot be changed. Acceptance helps you to move on and go with the flow. I can promise you that one of the happiest moments in your life will be when you find the courage to let go of what you can't change.

Another thing to accept is that you are really not missing out by not drinking alcohol. If life wasn't better sober, I would not have written this book. I've written it, not for self-healing, but for helping others. I was healed the second I accepted I was not in control. If my life was unmanageable sober, I would have gone back to drinking. So would all the other thousands of people who have called time on their drinking habits. If it was impossible, then it would not have been possible for me or anyone else. And to be honest, I was undressing last night and I suddenly thought "it's no big deal stopping drinking. It's only actually the thought that it's a big deal". The decision is the hardest part. The cure is the prize that just keeps unfolding in front of you every day; the change in your appearance and the balance in your mind.

#Sober Not Boring

If you change nothing, then nothing will change. If you change something, then something will change.

On top of the clear head, weight loss, sparkling eyes, fresh, younger looking skin, you will also be carrying around a supreme knowledge about what it means to live without suffering. The root of suffering is attachment according to Buddha and you are attached to the *thought* that alcohol is giving you pleasure.

How do you let go of attachment to things? Open your hands. Let them go. As the law of resistance states, stop trying. There are only really two reasons as to why we can't let something go and they are an attachment to the past or a fear for the future. Sometimes it is hard to let go of alcohol because we have done it for so long and because we are afraid of what the future will be like without it.

Sometimes just being aware of something, teaches you how to understand something.

Yasmin Mogahed describes attachment perfectly:

"Try not to confuse "attachment" with "love". Attachment is about fear and dependency, and has more to do with love of self than love of another. Love without attachment is the purest love because it isn't about what others can give you because you're empty. It is about what you can give others because you're already full".

How do we gain from within? We have to feel full from our own mind and heart.

"Put your hand on your heart, the old man said.

Inside you, there is a power, there are ideas, thoughts that no-one has ever thought of, there is the strength to love, purely and intensely, and to have someone love you back – there is the power to make people happy and make people laugh – its full compliments, and the power to change lives and futures. Don't ever forget that power, and don't ever give up on it" – Atticus

When you learn to master non-attachment you start to care less about what people think about you; you stop worrying and you become self-assured. The saying "cut loose" is a popular one I use on myself if I ever feel something or someone is bothering me. It's the *thought* that they are bothering me that I am attached to, therefore I imagine the thought as a rope attached to me then I cut it loose! It's an enlightening way to live. When I was drinking, the rope was literally around my neck and my hands were filled with yesterday's junk, hence it was impossible to cut loose.

"You've always had the power my dear; you just had to learn it for yourself".
Glinda – The Wizard of Oz.

ON BEING PRESENT

"One of the most tragic things I know about human nature is that all of us tend to put off living. We are all dreaming of some magical rose garden over the horizon – instead of enjoying the roses that are blooming outside our windows today". - Dale Carnegie

We all have desires and expectations and we compare the reality we have, which is miraculous and wondrous, with the reality we desire. This kind of attachment to a thought (of how we think something should be) as I have explained before, creates suffering. For me, the thing that I love about being sober is that life becomes all about the present moment. When we drink alcohol, we are always idealising about the future, when an event does not live up to our expectation, or day dream, we deal with this by idealising again. And so a vicious circle of drinking, fantasising and disappointment becomes a habit.

When we are caught up in the alcohol trap we are missing the now and thinking of the future or the past. When we are under the influence of alcohol, we like to complicate things when it is really quite simple; enjoy the present moment, just as it is. When you stop drinking, you will be more equipped to start living in the present and more importantly, enjoying every second.

One of the best methods to try when starting to practice living in the present moment is when you are washing a plate. Instead of rushing, start by focusing on your hand, slowly washing the plate. Look at the movement of your hand, the design of the plate and the bubbles moving with your hand. Once you master carrying out chores this way, you become much more grounded and life feels as though it has slowed down.

When you start to practice living in the moment, try not to label everything you look at because by doing this, you are still using your mind to search for a name and description for that which you are viewing and that in itself takes you away from the present moment.

Start to look at nature for what it really is, with no name and no label. Once you master this, nature starts to look different and begins to come alive. Trees, clouds and the sky start to be seen with only your eyes and this vision actually touches your heart and soul. There is beauty in silence. When the world is moving and your mind is still, you will see the truth and the truth of a single moment is miraculous. You will also start to see much further in front of you. By closing your mind, you open up your eyes and you literally start to see the wood on the trees and the green fields in the distance. Nature starts to come to life and looks brighter than ever before.

Be patient. When you look at something differently (with no labelling) it will become different. Believing is seeing (not the other way around). We see what we want to see or what we are used to seeing, because we are not properly looking; we have not been present for so long. Start to believe that there is so much more and the universe will start to show you so much more.

We can never be present when we drink alcohol in the way a problem drinker drinks alcohol. A normal drinker can enjoy the present moment because they are not thinking about their next drink, however with a problem drinker, the bad wolf becomes bigger and the strength of the wolf is such that it can be overcome only by spiritual power and being present is a powerful spiritual act.

When we look more closely at nature we develop a deeper understanding of the present moment and the miracle of the life we have been given.

When you are hung over, you may not realise it, but you are walking around in a self-absorbed fog, not noticing anyone or anything and your consciousness is expressing unhappiness. When you get through the first few weeks of alcohol free living, you feel and look more confident because you are not hiding behind any physical and mental pain. When you start caring about yourself, it is not selfish or self-absorbed, it is a quiet contentment and you start to express this outwardly without really trying. You start living in the moment and you start noticing the moment and realising that the moment is really all you have.

I no longer read newspapers and news and showbiz apps. Instead, I have focused on creative, uplifting and inspiring apps such as Pinterest. I am now an avid pinner! I have come to realise that photographs of animals make me feel really happy and beautiful images of landscapes really uplift me. I suppose I am truly getting to know myself, unmasked and uncloaked; I have come to understand what really feeds my soul. And this is precisely how you fill your soul up to the point where it is overflowing - you get to know what makes you feel happy and you keep on doing it - "Know thyself" - Socrates

When once, the sun rising during a drive to work would have caused me undue stress; it now takes my breath away. Not just the size and beauty of the sun, but the effect it has on the colour of the sky and the landscape surrounding it.

When was the last time something took your breath away while you were drinking? The only thing that stunned me at times was how quickly my bottle was emptying!

One of my favourite sayings is "Look with wonder at that which lies before you". I was telling my friend and Daughter this saying one day last Christmas and just as I finished, we turned a corner and right in front of us was the most beautiful ice sculpture of Tinkerbell. Further up the road was Rudolph, some angel wings, a diamond and more! It truly was the most magical day and the saying "look with wonder at that which lies before you" is now set into the alarm screen of my phone, pasted in my journals, and pinned on my mood boards.

A WONDERFUL EXERCISE FOR PRACTISING THE ACT OF BEING PRESENT

This is a fantastic exercise for practising the act of being present, made all the more beautiful by your choice of objects.

You will need:

100 buttons or other small objects

1 decorative box

I chose buttons because my sister had hundreds to choose from and deciding which hundred to choose was a delightful experience in itself. You can also use small pieces of material, shells, pebbles, crystals. My box is a beautiful, hand crafted jewellery box and again, I chose this specifically for my button exercise.

The objective is to place the pile in front of you and slowly and meticulously, transfer each button into the box. Do not do this on auto pilot; you are quite simply witnessing an act unfolding in front of your eyes. This is the opposite of auto pilot and you are completely conscious of every single moment.

Do not count the buttons as this means you are "thinking". Do not rush, as this defeat's the object of savouring each moment. If you start thinking about needing to buy milk, you are not present. If you start silently commenting on the colour of each button, you are not present. The aim is to entirely clear your mind of any thoughts until you get to the stage of detachment whereby your hand does not look or appear to be part of you. You are simply a witness.

With daily practice, you will start to strengthen your will and your skill at living in the present moment. It can be difficult at first, but the more you do it the better you become and the stronger your resolve will become, believe me.

#Sober Not Boring

Not only can I attest to this, but it has been scientifically proven. Studies have shown that the pre-frontal cortex of the brain, which controls emotional responses and stores your plans and impulses, is strengthened when you practice this kind of exercise, which means you are better equipped to deal with stresses and less prone to impulsive action, such as buying alcohol after a bad day at work.

SELF- DISCIPLINE

"If you learn self-control, you can master anything" - Unknown

The aim of this chapter is to help you find and maintain other ways of strengthening your resolve and keeping the bad wolf at bay. Remember the wolf you feed always wins? The seed you focus on always flowers? To master the art of being present, if only for a few minutes a day, is the start of strengthening your will and in turn, strengthening your resolve. "It is during our darkest moments, that we must focus to see the light" is a Buddha quote I love about being present and focusing on the spirit within that shines the light on your path.

To focus, takes will. To sit up straight takes will. To get up in the morning takes will. Your will is like a muscle, you can train it to get stronger. I know; I have trained mine very well and I would not be the person I am today doing the things I am doing, had I not strengthened my will and in turn, my resolve. Have you ever woken up the morning after drinking and said "never again". Not just said it, but actually really meant it, only for it to get to five o clock and you are straight out the door and heading to the shop on the way home? Your will was tired and weakened as the day went on, just as your muscles were. So how do you strengthen it?

The button exercise is a very good way of learning to be present and strengthening your will.

Standing up and doing something the very second you think about it (cleaning, making a cup of tea, having a clear out) is another good way of strengthening your will. The Nike saying "Just do it" sums this up perfectly. There is a voice that sits above your spirit voice and this is the voice of the will. The one that says "pick the post off the floor before you make a coffee" or "watch out for the cat that's about to run in front of the car". Don't ignore this voice as ignoring it leads to procrastination. Acting on it becomes a habit and you get things done. It's quite simple. The more you get done, the more you get done.

#Sober Not Boring

Meditation strengthens your will. By meditating you are training the brain to focus and resist the urge to wander. Research shows that after just three days of practising meditation for ten minutes, your brain will be able to focus better, you will be less stressed and you will have more energy. I am a huge fan of meditation and astral projection and have some lovely meditations to help strengthen your will, in my second book "Just the Tonic".

Keeping your surroundings clean and tidy strengthens your will. In one study, some participants were taken to a tidy laboratory while others were placed in a messy one. Those in the messy lab exhibited less self-control. They ate less healthy snacks and gave up quicker on tasks.

This takes us on to an even better study you may have heard about called Rat Park. This was a study into drug addiction in the 1970's by a Canadian psychologist called Bruce K Alexander. Alexander's hypothesis was that drugs do not cause addiction, and that the apparent addiction to opiate drugs commonly observed in lab rats exposed to it (opium) is attributable to their living conditions, and not to any addictive property of the drug itself. He found that rats isolated in cramped metal cages, tethered to self-injection apparatus showed that severely distressed animals, like severely distressed people, will relieve their distress pharmacologically if they can. When the rats were moved to a purpose built, spacious Rat Park, with an abundance of food, balls and wheels to play on, and given a choice between plain tap water and water laced with morphine, for the most part, they chose the plain water, proving that their surroundings made it easier to wean themselves off the morphine *and* not go back to it.

A routine strengthens your will. By creating a routine, you are creating a good habit and you are more likely to minimise the number of temptations you are faced with. Once you have a routine, you don't have to worry about what you should be doing at any given moment. Even now, I still pick up my daily shopping during my lunch hour. That was a routine I developed in the early days and I have still kept it up. That said, once I had made my decision to stop, I could quite happily walk along the alcohol aisle or sit with a friend who was drinking alcohol, but these little routines helped strengthen my resolve and that is what we are trying to do at this stage.

I can vouch a million percent for the next thing I am about to say and I am the last person who would have believed this: The best way to strengthen your will and stay off alcohol is by exercise. If the will is like a muscle then it figures that exercise would be the best way to strengthen it.

Let's also just remind ourselves of the definition of recovery:

"A return to a normal state of health, mind or strength".

"The action or process of regaining possession or control of something lost or stolen".

The reason I strongly believe that exercise is so important in your recovery (even though it may be the last thing on your mind) is that when you start to see your body changing for the better, your resolve becomes strengthened. The longer you abstain from alcohol, the easier it becomes. The longer you abstain from alcohol, the younger and fitter you start to look. It really is that simple.

Drinking had developed into a habit therefore exercise will become that too. I promise. You are more than capable of building a habit. Ok, alcohol is an addictive drug, therefore it is easier to build, but once you witness the changes to your mood, your skin, your body, you will want to do everything possible to keep feeding these changes and exercise really is the magic formula here.

When you think about exercising, don't think about treadmills, bikes, spinning classes and sweating. That thought in itself is enough to put any new bunny off. I've done all that before, many years ago, and I hated every minute of it. I did it purely to keep my weight down and because friends were looking so fit and healthy (following the crowd). And nearly always on the way home, I would pick up some cans of cider and get my high from them instead.

#Sober Not Boring

I have always envied gym bunnies, but I used to think that even for them; going to the gym was a miserable struggle that they felt obliged to do to keep their weight down. I also used to think that about sober people – not drinking was a daily struggle and you would spend the rest of your life wanting to drink. How wrong I was on both thoughts! It's hard to get started but once you do, it's hard to stop, and I'm talking about weight training. And by weight training I don't mean body building (however weight training is certainly brain building). I mean training my body with weights; lifting heavy things, lifting my own body weight. Training with weights, results in retraining your mind to act with precision and focus. It also strengthens your will (which as I've already said is like a muscle).

Weight training takes up an hour every morning of being truly grounded (unless you are hanging from a bar) and truly present. You cannot lift a heavy weight whilst thinking about the past. I have seen a trainer lift a heavy beanbag type weight into the air and then throw it onto the ground with some force, and I am certain this would be a good exercise for stamping out negative memories of the past. However, I much prefer the slow, focussed precision required to lift a heavy weight. You've spent a long time carrying a heavy weight with no gain; it's now time to start lifting heavy weights with a lot of gain.

You will gain:

A strong will (that lasts all day long and well into the evening)
Muscle
Good posture
Discipline
Precision
Focus
Nerves of steel
Brainpower
Routine
Ideas
Creativity
Respect (for yourself and from others)

Envy (from others)
Drive
Determination
A completely new outlook on life
The list goes on.

The thought of going back to a life of drinking alcohol is inconceivable to me now and this feeling came to me after only a couple of months of giving up alcohol and starting to weight train. The difference abstaining from alcohol this time around compared to other times is down to finally understanding that:

EVERYTHING had to change within me. I HAD to be the change I wanted to create.

I would feel mortified if I found myself unable to keep up with the morning routine because something so fattening and poisoning had a grip over me again. It is a no brainer for me now and it can be like that for you too. You may not believe it yet, but the clue to getting going is getting started.

I am the last person on earth who would ever get up earlier than I needed to and this was not just due to having a hangover. From as far back as I can remember, I always used to say "I'm not a morning person" but apparently, there is no such thing! We become what we say we are, therefore I have now become a morning person.

The biggest antidote to a weak will is to start getting up an hour earlier in the midst of winter. When you can do this, you have strengthened your will and without realising it, you have strengthened your resolve.

The other benefit of getting up earlier is how proud you feel each time you do it, and just like stopping drinking, the more you do it, the easier it becomes. If it was too difficult, I would have given up and gone back to my old ways. The desire to change must be stronger than your desire to

#Sober Not Boring

stay the same remember and once you see your face, body and mind changing, your desire to hold onto these results, keeps you going.

Watching the light unfolding with a clear head on my way to the gym is a feeling I can't describe. I never once thought I would enjoy life again, let alone so early in the morning and I sometimes have to pinch myself at how far I have come. In just three days, the alcohol addiction had left my body. In just three weeks, the clouds started to lift and in just three months, my life, my body and my mind were transformed. I promise you that if I can do this then so can you.

It really is amazing what a change of mind-set can do for you. There is a feeling I get at the gym at 7am in the morning, which must express itself to onlookers and that is this: I am dedicated and I am committed. Not just to getting fit, but to staying sober. No-one would guess the battles I have gone through to get to where I am. And because I feel this on the inside, I express this on the outside and I keep on living up to it and the feeling just keeps on getting stronger. There is nothing more rewarding than working out because you love your body and not because you hate it. I don't work out to punish my body for what I've put into it the night before; I work out to nourish and reward my body for keeping me alive. I look at my breast cancer scars and remind myself of the way in which my body healed itself after surgery and how I took this process for granted and abused it in return. I hope that every cell of me knows completely and utterly, just how much I love the miracle of life and how thankful I am.

Don't wait for an illness to remind you of the value of life.

MORE BENEFITS OF EXERCISE

'Sore from a workout is better than being hungover after a party" - Unknown

Alcohol triggers the release of dopamine which is a chemical that produces feelings of satisfaction. It also increases the production of the brains natural painkiller endorphin which scientists think could be the means by which the brain becomes trained to crave. So if alcohol leads to the production of endorphins and dopamine within the human body, giving rise to feelings of pleasure, general well being and the reduction of pain - when we take away the alcohol, do we take away these feelings? Not if we exercise. If we exercise, we can actually magnify these feelings. Once you see results, exercise becomes an addiction in itself and you keep getting these feelings.

But it's easier to get these feelings whilst sitting on a sofa with a bottle of wine. It is indeed, but what comes after that? You know only too well. Progress is impossible without change and unless you change, you will keep getting what you are getting. I don't recall alcohol making me feel better, boosting my mood, boosting my brainpower, reducing my anxiety, reducing my waistline, increasing my concentration, giving me amazing sleep, making me look younger.

So apart from the list of gains in the previous chapter, exercise also gives you all the things we *thought* alcohol gave us but actually took away from us.

Your body will reward you once start exercising and good habits are much more rewarding than bad habits!

As for the extra brainpower: I can't begin to explain what weight training has done for my ability to concentrate, focus and learn. Surely that's what life is all about. I missed so much when I was locked in the dark cage; so very much. But it's never too late. It doesn't bother me one little bit that I have only discovered this at the age of forty three. You are

#Sober Not Boring

always where you are supposed to be to learn the lessons you are supposed to learn and I really hope you are at that place too.

WHAT DO I TELL PEOPLE?

"The more you love your decisions, the less you need others to love them"-Unknown

Once you stop drinking you realise that most people don't actually care. They can't generally tell if your soda and lime contains vodka or not. *Thinking* there would be too much peer pressure on you if you stopped, was just another untruth the bad wolf fed you. However there will always be someone or two, who will undermine your decision and try to make you start doubting it. These are usually the people with alcohol issues themselves.

Don't forget that when you make a big change to your lifestyle, this will unsettle other people, especially when you start losing weight and looking younger. In my experience, friends started explaining their drinking to me as though I was judging them. I would confidently clarify that it was my drinking I was worried about, not theirs.

The less concerned I am about other people and what they may or may not think about me, the happier I am. When I started to "cut loose" from the bad wolf (ego) and started moving forward, freedom and joy appeared with very little effort. The less attached (to thoughts) I became, the more my life started to transform.

Sometimes people who drink have never tried life without it, or have never even imagined trying. They will start to play down your drinking and tell you it wasn't that bad. They will assume that you won't be able to have fun anymore, that you will be boring. How can they profess to know about something they have never experienced? Don't forget that this is your road and your journey. Remind yourself often that you don't have to do what everyone else is doing. You have set your sights on where you are going and you have said goodbye to where you have been. And only YOU know where you have been. Don't explain. If someone says you have changed, what they are really saying is that you have stopped living life their way, or the way they think you should be living it.

I would like to say that when asked why you don't drink, the truth prevails. However this is not always that easy; plus when you first start out, you may still be testing a life without alcohol and you may not feel ready to admit to others that alcohol was becoming a problem for you.

The following is a list of examples I have given when asked why I don't drink:

My medication (tamoxifen) makes me feel sick when I drink;
I've got a busy day tomorrow, I want a clear head;
I'm determined to lose weight;
I've just started weight training, heavy weights and hangovers don't mix;
I'm driving;
I'm on a health kick;

The longer you go sober, the more self-assured you become, therefore very few people actually ask you, plus they can see how much fun you are having without a drink. Trust me. Some people have actually asked me the next day if I had a hangover. They hadn't even noticed I wasn't drinking!

SUPPORT

"What I can do is offer myself, wholehearted and present, to walk with the people I love through the fear and the mess. That's all any of us can do. That's what we're here for" – Shauna Niequist

When I phoned Lifeline, I already knew the answer and I knew I had cracked it the minute I admitted to myself I was no longer in control and asked for help. That in itself was the breakthrough I had been looking for.

A few months before I stopped drinking, I went to the Doctor to ask for the anti-smoking medication Champix. I was sick and tired of smoking and quite frankly, I could no longer afford it. Plus I thought that Champix may help me stop drinking too. It didn't but what happened was this. The Doctor laughed and said "I'm not just handing that over to you! You have to prove you are committed to stopping and go to a stop smoking clinic". I took the phone number but I was furious, and the first thing I wanted to do when I left the surgery, was light up a cigarette. But I didn't. And the reason I didn't was because I had convinced myself that this was the day I would start treatment and stop smoking. And this was the day I had told my daughter I would stop smoking too. I had psyched myself up. The power of the subconscious mind! I had basically said to my subconscious mind "we stop smoking today" and it took me at my word, as it does. So for weeks, I travelled to the clinic every Tuesday after work and the one to one therapy system completely worked for me. I did buy myself wine on the way back to my car as a reward afterwards though.

The very same thing happened with alcohol. I asked for help (thinking they might give me a magic pill) and they gave me the number for Lifeline.

The point of this chapter is to let you know that there is so much help out there; you just have to ask for it. And by asking for it, I suppose I mean, give yourself permission to seek it. You are not weak for asking, you are strong and intelligent for asking. The people that will help you are ordinary people like you and me, who have been where we have been and they know that change can be achieved and embraced. There are

#Sober Not Boring

people who have been to even darker places than me and have transformed their lives.

It's an illusion to think that problem drinkers are only the ones who drink first thing in the morning, drink throughout the day and sleep on park benches at night. No, problem drinkers are just like you and me with one thing in common; they drink too much alcohol and it causes problems in their lives. Maybe the person on the park bench was once like me and didn't ask for help soon enough.

The AA is an amazing, spiritual organisation and the only reason I have never attended any meetings is because I believe in labelling yourself the thing that you wish to become – sober, successful, slim, happy etc; rather than the thing that you are. I don't want to ever give power back to that thing, therefore I prefer to draw a line under it and move on.

The AA is not a religion and it is not linked to any religion. It is a very spiritual, harmonious group and the one thing I do think would be great for me is that I would meet like-minded people. And maybe, one day I will venture in, however I will stand up and say "I AM April and I AM sober".

The reason I attend Lifeline is to show commitment – to myself. I am only there for ten minutes every four weeks now. I would like to volunteer there and become a counsellor myself and that is one of my goals. I do it for a routine and to make a pre-commitment. I do it in case there are any strange feelings I come across that I want to share with my counsellor. I do it because I feel proud of myself. I do it to offload any personal issues and run things by my counsellor. She can't tell me what to do about a certain life situation, but just telling her usually gives me the answer. I do it because I like my counsellor and she used the AA six years ago. I do it to talk about the weather; we rarely talk about alcohol. I will always remember her saying to me after three months "you look amazing". And I knew it was because I felt amazing; everything was coming together. It's a nice place with nice people and no-one judges you.

GOAL- DREAMING

"You are never too old to set another goal or to dream a new dream" – *CS Lewis*

So much of my time drinking was spent daydreaming and fantasising; I'm surprised I never came up with an amazing plot for a novel.

A fantasy is exactly that, a fantasy. Fantasies are unachievable and as I've said before, no-one says no in fantasy and there is always a happy ending. Deep down, I think I have always been a fantasist; definitely a daydreamer anyway. You can still daydream sober; the difference is that your daydreams are realistic and much more achievable because you are in a level frame of mind.

I now prefer to call my daydreaming "goal dreaming" because that is exactly what I am doing. Dreaming about my goals and working out ways in which I can achieve them. When you wake up the next day and still feel excited about your goal dream, then you must pursue it. We are all born with a talent and once you chose hope, anything is possible. "The meaning of life is to find your gift; the purpose of life is to give it away" Joy J Golliver. We all have something to give. We've just got to work out what it is and start to believe we can achieve it. Again, it's about listening to the voice of spirit inside you and you will know deep down what you want to do.

Before I stopped drinking I realised I didn't have a goal. I feel embarrassed about this now. I had achieved very little in my life apart from having a beautiful daughter and positively overcoming breast cancer, but I didn't actually have a goal.

If you put a blank envelope in a post box it won't go anywhere. If you put an address on it but no stamp it may reach its destination in time, but if you put an address *and* a stamp on it, it will reach its destination with near certainty. So my advice is to make a list of your goals, put a stamp on them and start goal dreaming about how you intend to reach them.

#Sober Not Boring

You don't have to have it all figured out in order to start moving forward, but goals certainly help.

When we were younger, we all had dreams and hopes. Then we started to follow the crowd, then alcohol got in the way, then we got complacent and depressed and started working to live. What happened to our dreams? We became overpowered by the bad wolf and we started to believe that external circumstances were the cause of our unhappy lives. We didn't realise that the cause was with our *thoughts* about our lives. We started to lack direction and drive and we stopped making goals let alone putting a stamp on them. Our drive was focussed on chasing feelings instead of chasing dreams.

The next time you daydream, ask yourself if it is realistic. If not, then switch to a more realistic goal dream and then tick it off your list!

Before I go to sleep, I do still allow myself a little fantasy about the knight in shining armour, but not before I have reflected on the day and reviewed all that I have done to get closer to my goals.

I write much more about goal dreaming and finding happiness in my second book JUST THE TONIC.

BOREDOM

"Boredom: the desire for desires" – Leo Tolstoy

I drank because I was bored. I drank because I wanted a better life, so I fantasised about a better life. Boring people get bored, that's why they talk about the past and fantasise about the future; they are bored. They don't know how to live in the present. When you stop drinking, you instantly create a better life. When I look at all the things I have achieved *just* by stopping drinking alcohol; weight loss, bright eyes, younger looking skin, hobbies, health, an amazing outlook on life (and the life ahead of me which I embrace and feel excited about) I can't possibly allow myself to get bored.

There is no time to be bored in a world as beautiful as this. You have simply forgotten. If you can't see the wonder of the things you have been given for free, then the fault lies in yourself. Maybe you prefer to live on the dark side. Or maybe the dark side is all that you have known for so long. With practice, being present and using gratitude when you notice something beautiful *will* become second nature.

Sometimes, it's ok to sit and do nothing at all. In fact, I would strongly recommend this in the early days. Your body is recovering from the damage that regular use of alcohol has caused and your mind is recovering from all the tabs that were open at one time; the anger, pain and suffering it endured.

I can't actually say that I got bored early on. I got busy. I definitely think that boredom was a visitor when I was drinking, but not when I stopped drinking. I think I used to beat myself up when I felt bored or lazy when I was drinking, whereas now, I embrace being lazy. I love lighting my candles and my incense and relaxing. It feels different now. It's the bad wolf that gets bored and searches for interesting thoughts and now that I have dissolved the bad wolf, everything I think is interesting to me because everything I think is about how I can learn and move forward. It's no longer about thinking about the past to amuse myself or changing the story, I'm now thinking about the present moment and what I can do to grow.

Here are some things I have invited into my life (to stay) now that I have stopped drinking:

Sunshine, clouds, rain, health, air, art, music, passion, creativity, singing, dancing, mother nature, rest, play, memories, this moment, sunrise, sunset, birds, herbs, flowers, laughter, health, exercise, sleep, books, writing, meditation, scrapbooks, friends.

Here are some suggestions for you to unlock the unused creative potential you have inside you:

Start a journal – treat yourself to a beautiful notebook and write, write, write! Write down all the things you are grateful for. How about starting with "I am grateful for having the courage to confront my problems". Write about your recovery so that you can go back and remind yourself just how far you have come.

Read – you can't get more present than you are when you read a book. The other benefits are that your imagination is being stimulated, your reading speed increases, your focus and ability to concentrate is strengthened and so is your will. You don't have to read novels, I love anything that feeds my soul and fills me up - art books, photography books, fitness books, spiritual books, and self help books.

Learn new exercises - sometimes a whole evening will go by when I'm watching and learning new exercise techniques on you tube. I have become addicted to self care and self improvement. It's a great feeling watching something you are going to learn from but even better when your vision isn't blurred. I have learnt many a new exercise from watching you tube clips – type in exercises for women (or men) using your own body weight.

Learn to draw – some people are born with a gift for drawing and some people are born with a pre-disposition towards alcoholism, but both things can be learned. There are a lot of ways to learn how to draw and paint including books, apps and you tube clips.

Start a scrapbook – I adore scrapbooks, and journals; anything I can stick inspirational pictures, postcards or articles in. Each page holds a special memory for me, just as photo albums do.   Every now and again, I download photos from my phone and stick them in an album. The memory seems to be brought back to life when it's printed rather than on a screen.

Start a gratitude jar – every time you notice something to be grateful for, write it on a piece of paper and put it in your jar. Every now and then you can empty your jar, read the miracles you saw, stick them in your scrapbook and then start to fill the jar again.

Make a mood board – I am a huge fan of mood boards and have a few collages put together of my goals, ideal man, body inspirations, quotes, thoughts. It should be called a motivation board really.

Get pinning – I am huge fan of Pinterest. This is a website that allows you to "pin" things online, just as you would on a real life pin board. I have so many inspirational boards that I would love to press a button and print every pin out and then stick them on my own live mood boards. Instead, I have filled my second book "Just The Tonic" with uplifting quotes, thoughts and exercises to help you stop drinking.

Learn – don't wait for something terrible to happen to you before you learn spiritual laws, healing, prayer, art, philosophy, metaphysics and meditation – "educating yourself does not mean that you were stupid in the first place; it means that you are intelligent enough to know that there is plenty left to learn" – Melanie Joy

Your perspective is always limited by how much you know. Expand your knowledge and you will transform your mind. Knowledge is power and anything that can become more powerful than ego, the bad wolf, can only be a positive thing.

#Sober Not Boring

Collect recipes – then start to cook or bake the recipes.

Make jewellery – Etsy is a fantastic arts and crafts website where you can gain inspiration for making all kinds of things. I started making and selling jewellery last year and got all my inspiration and skills from suppliers on Etsy. It's an inspirational website for revealing your hidden creative potential.

Make clothes – again use Etsy for inspiration and buy fabric from here too. The suppliers are from all over the world!

Do something new – with all the spare time and money you will have, start to plan to do something you've never done before.

I love the following quote: "when was the last time you did something for the first time?" I think it says it all really.

It is unbelievable how much creative potential we have stored within us. I can't believe that at forty three I have only just discovered how to start tapping into the creative side of my brain. I feel excited all the time. There is so much more to do in the evenings and weekends. I never thought for a second I could ever feel like this.

Was I really depressed for so long? It's a terrifying thought that alcohol created such a dark cloak over an already dark cage. The desire for knowledge and creativity is overwhelming at times and I want more! I know that my transformation is a combination of saying goodbye to alcohol and hello to exercise. I always believed that the people who felt like this had excess energy, however it is this zest for life that gives you this energy. I have glanced at books about unlocking your hidden potential but I never believed I had any, so I never read them. I want to teach people how to have this zest for life and the starting point is to take away the alcohol and replace it with exercise. Understand the power of the subconscious mind, start making affirmations a habit and start making goals.

The zest will follow!

FORGIVENESS

"I love you, I'm sorry, please forgive me, thank you" – Dr Len

Loving yourself is the greatest way to improve yourself and it starts with forgiving yourself. As you know, I am big believer in moving on; I know what self-pity and living in the past can do to your health and how much it can compound addiction.

Forgiving yourself is a bit like acceptance. You have to let go of what has happened to you and forgive yourself in the process. Only you know what you have been through, how you have spoken to yourself and acted in your times of struggle. A nice quote I remind myself of is: "remember when you forgive, you heal. And when you let go, you grow".

I am big believer in Hawaiian healing techniques and have been since I studied Reiki whilst undergoing chemotherapy. My Reiki teacher taught me the technique of "Ho'oponopono" which was discovered by a therapist in Hawaii who cured a complete ward of criminally insane patients, without ever seeing them, just by looking at photographs of them and saying: "I love you, I'm sorry, please forgive me, thank you". It's a complex study but he basically took full responsibility for these patients and had a view that we are all one of the same. So he started to work on himself by saying this mantra and in turn, the patients started to recover. This is the power of forgiveness. I say these words to myself often; I never forget.

I love the Hawaiian culture so much that when I stopped drinking I had a tattoo done along my right foot saying "I Mua" which is Hawaiian for "To go forth". This sums up the whole process of drawing a line under the past and moving forward, being re-born, resurrecting, I mua. It means so much to me and it's a daily reminder that the only way I'm going is forward.

TURNING BACK

"I can't go back to yesterday because I was a different person then". Alice in Wonderland

When we make big changes in our lives, our emotional and physical states change too. With enough time and patience, they will balance themselves out. I promise you this.

Never interpret feeling unsettled, bored or tired for unhappiness or for making the wrong decision. Never doubt the decision you have made. Deep down you already know the truth, never doubt it. Never forget the darkness in the cage where you have just escaped from. Do not look back. If you look back, it will never seem as bad as it was. Never look back into the dead past I say.

Relapse is really not an option. If you give up now, then what was the point of everything? I will not sugar coat anything here. Alcohol has sugar coated itself for years, I will not do that to you. I will only speak the truth, from experience of despair, hope and then freedom. Your life and the contents of your thoughts were a mess when you were drinking. Never lose sight of that. Never forget where you were and you will be less likely to go back.

Every now and again I will get a reminder of how bad things were and I sometimes can't comprehend that I was in that place for so long.

Stumbling on the way back to bed after going to the toilet can give me a sharp reminder of where I was. A stumble now is just purely because it is dark and I am half asleep; a stumble then was a pitiful sight, collapsing into bed, heavy hearted; heavy everything, telling myself how worthless and stupid I was.

Even now, if I miss my footing going to sit on the sofa, the first thing I say to my daughter is "I've not been drinking; I just lost my balance". Of course, she knows I haven't been drinking – a stumble is quite normal, but what gave away the fact it was drink related was the smell of alcohol, the bloodshot eyes, the vacant look, the slurring, the hopelessness and then of course the stumble.

If you give up and think that you can do it all again at a later date, your resolve will be much weaker than that light bulb moment when you found the key. Trust me. You may never get that back again and you will spend the rest of your life in a cage. The torment of living on and off the wagon is hell; the guilt and shame you feel on waking up in the morning feels much worse than the days when you were drinking full time. I can assure you of this. Plus, you will nearly always drink more if you relapse. The change in your face and body will be sudden and you will feel truly rotten.

Controlling something that already controls you is impossible. You have waded too far in. If you are still in the shallow end then you can probably rein it back, but once you get in too deep, you can't. The only thing you can do is wait for the tide to go out, dry yourself off and go back to the shore; and don't look back as you are not going that way. If you go back after a period of drying out thinking that you are back in control, you will find that the tide comes in much, much quicker and you will drown. I have been there many times. Acceptance that you can't is really the only thing that keeps you on the beach, enjoying the sunshine.

I even went through a phase where I resigned myself to the fact that I may spend the rest of my life in the cage. Thank god something changed and I made that switch and flipped the coin over.

Sometimes when I pass a beer garden I feel a twinge of melancholy and I think "Why can't I just have one nice, cold pint of cider?" and then I remember that there was never a time when I would just have one.

So it goes back to acceptance and letting it be. I can have a full fat pint of Coke, or an ice cold soda with lime and better still, look exactly the same at the end of the night as I did at the beginning. I can remember everything and I've probably laughed the most! We must learn to unblock the condition that drinking is fun and people who don't drink are boring.

#Sober Not Boring

Drinking was not fun for us. It might have been in the early days, but something changed; we became addicted and we lost control.

We think that people are laughing and joking because they are drinking alcohol. This is not true. People are laughing and joking because the sun is out, they are not at work and they are enjoying themselves.

Towards the end of the night, I am still laughing, however the drinkers are incoherent, repetitive and sometimes crying. And the next day when I am up watching the day unfold and filling my soul, they are probably still in bed, feeling terrible and wasting precious time.

April Green

WHEN THINGS GO WRONG

"When things go wrong, don't go with them" – Elvis Presley

Once you've made the decision to stop drinking, the strength comes from within you when faced with a difficult life situation, not from without. The bottle will break you in times of struggle, whereas the spirit will carry you. We were conditioned to believe that a stiff drink would make us stronger whereas the opposite is true.

One of my favourite poems is "Footprints in the Sand" and this explains how the spirit within you, will carry you through times of trouble:

"One night a man had a dream.
He dreamed he was walking along the beach with the Lord.
Across the sky flashed scenes from his life.
For each scene, he noticed two sets of footprints in the sand;
One belonging to him and the other to the Lord.
When the last scene of his life flashed before him, he looked back at the footprints in the sand.
He noticed that many times along the path of his life, there was only one set of footprints.
He also noticed that it happened at the very lowest and saddest times in his life.
This really bothered him and he questioned the Lord about it.
"Lord, you said that once I decide to follow you, you'd walk with me all the way.
But I have noticed that during the most troublesome times in my life, there is only one set of footprints.
I don't understand why when I needed you the most you would leave me"
The Lord replied:
"My son, my precious child
I love you and would never leave you.
During your times of trial and suffering,

When you only see one set of footprints,
It was then that I carried you".

Remember that there is a voice deep within you that speaks to you when you are silent, when you are in pain, when you are suffering and this is your spirit, your true self and this is the thing that will never leave you and will carry you through life. This is the voice that has already saved you by telling you that you are drinking too much, that you are worth so much more and by helping you find a way out.

If you want to know what your future holds, just tell yourself what you want; write it down and set a goal. Become your own fortune teller. When things are sent to try you, you will not get lost or thrown off route, because you have your goal to reach. In moments like this, stand still and try and find the blessing (or lesson) in what has been sent. It may be that you change your path because of this storm, but remember that ships come in on a calm sea.

SOME SOBERING THOUGHTS

"I want to spend the rest of my life alive" - Unknown

In the early days and for as long as you can get away with it - sleep.

Sleep, laughter and comfort. You have punished yourself enough. It is time to treat yourself like the little child within you who has been crying out for help. Feed yourself healthy food and make sure you spend time outside. Put yourself to bed early and take naps often. Nourish yourself like a child because this child is you and you can now begin to grow in to the person you were born to become.

At the beginning, focus on the three threes: 3 days for the physical addiction to leave your body; 3 weeks for the depression to lift and 3 months for the transformation to become visible.

A term the AA use to be the watchman at the gate is, HALT. Hungry, angry, lonely, tired. I used to be all of these things when I drank. I always had an emptiness I was searching to fill. Sadly, I used alcohol. Be aware of these four feelings. Snack often, get enough sleep, meditate away any anger, flip the coin over and look for laughter, and sleep if you are tired. As Buddha said "this too will pass".

A word on anger. In the early days I felt angry sometimes, usually in the evening. I think it is your body's way of asking for an outlet when it used to receive alcohol or it's the bad wolf waking up and wanting to be fed. Just be aware of this emotion and don't feed him. Feed your soul instead.

If you are single, sober sex is daunting and if you feel you need a drink before you can have sex for the first time with someone, then I would say that you are not ready to have sex with that person. Just because you had sex on date one, two or three when you were drinking doesn't mean to say that's how it should be now. You are a different person now. Fall in love differently. And love shouldn't hurt; if it does, cut loose.

#Sober Not Boring

It takes time to build up your self-esteem. Getting sober is the greatest thing you can do for yourself. Exercise comes second to that. Walk tall even if you are feeling vulnerable. Start to express high self-esteem and you will command a different level of respect from others without having to say anything. "You teach people how to treat you by what you allow, what you stop, and what you reinforce".

Those closest to you (especially your children) will start to follow your example and become more disciplined without needing to be reminded.

Guilt and shame diminish when you start respecting yourself.

If you are ever in doubt as to who is talking to you, ego or spirit, then ego is the voice of doubt, fear, and anger and spirit is the voice of you. It is the voice that uses your name not the voice that calls you names.

Drinking is diluting your creativity.

If you haven't yet linked alcohol as the cause of the way you behave and think, then you are bottling up the truth.

Your soul knows exactly what to do and that is heal itself. The hard part is keeping the bad wolf tamed.

The bad wolf is weakened without alcohol, but it is still there. Keep it in check at all times. If it rises, turn your attention to the present moment and look with wonder at that which lies before you.

"You must learn to get in touch with the innermost essence of your being. This true essence is beyond the ego. It is fearless; it is free; it is immune to criticism; it does not fear any challenge. It is beneath no-one, superior to no-one, and full of magic, mystery and enchantment" Deepak Chopra

Keep your eye on the prize. Every day. Always.

Stop escaping from life. Escape from the cage, but not from life. Stop rushing away the now.

April Green

There are three businesses in this world – your business, my business and the Universes business. We can't control the weather or earthquakes so why try and control the business of other people. Mind your own business and only your own business.

Looking in a mirror sober, feels much better than looking in a mirror drunk, or worst still, hung over.

Time heals but time spent healing yourself first, heals everything else.

Sober summers last longer and the sun seems to shine brighter.

You eat less when you are sober.

Christmas dinner tastes better sober and feeling bloated becomes a thing of the past.

Being in control of your mind and your weight and your emotions is a wonderful feeling.

Sober New Year resolutions change from giving something up, to starting something new.

The best thing for me about being sober - I have stopped being boring!

#Sober Not Boring

A HOPEFUL THOUGHT

I hope that when you close this book, you begin a new chapter in your life.

I hope you feel reassured that there is a magical, enchanting life to be had without alcohol and you completely deserve to be part of it.

You see, there is a garden waiting for you inside. There are seeds of hope to be planted. There is growth about to happen. It may take time, but there are buds on your trees and they are about to start flowering.

I hope you have the courage to go and have a look.

I hope you visit your garden daily and focus on its beauty, so that it begins to flourish.

I hope you understand that it gets easier to look after day by day.

And I hope that if things go wrong, you have the courage to go back to your garden, pull out all the weeds and start all over again.

April Green

(sobernotboring@outlook.com)

Printed in Great Britain
by Amazon